# FACTS &

ABOU

# PRESIDENTS OF THE UNITED STATES OF AMERICA

## For Curious Kids!

FIVE MILE PUBLICATIONS

# Contents

# Facts & Stories About The Presidents Of The United States Of America For Curious Kids!

# George Washington

**Born:**
Feb 22, 1732

**Birthplace:**
Popes Creek, Virginia

**Presidency:**
1789 - 1797

**Died:**
Dec 14, 1799

George Washington was born on February 22, 1732, in a small farm in Virginia. Back then, the United States wasn't even a country, instead it was a colony of the United Kingdom, the place where George's parents emigrated from! As a colony, the UK had control over American lands. Young George spent his days exploring the outdoors, riding horses, and helping his family grow tobacco and wheat on their farm, which helped the family become wealthy. George's father passed away when he was just eleven years old, so he had to grow up pretty quickly and take on the responsibilities his father once had. He didn't go to a fancy school, but he taught himself a lot by reading books and observing the world around him.

George learned the importance of honesty, hard work, and courage - values that would guide him throughout his life. At just 17 years old, George got his first job as a skilled surveyor, mapping the land around him. Soon after, he would begin a military career, protecting the interests of the colony and by 1755, left the army as a hero. Here, George would continue his life as a farmer, growing tobacco and gaining wealth.

But, over time, George knew he had a greater destiny. During the 1760s, troubles between the British rulers and the American colonies started. After seeing unjust rules and taxes that put the British at an advantage, George felt strongly that the Americans should have the right to govern themselves, free from British rule, so he joined the cause for independence.

When the American Revolution began, George was chosen to lead the Continental Army against the British. His task was not easy, as his soldiers were not professional soldiers like the British army was. They were ordinary people - farmers, blacksmiths, and teachers who had one common goal - they believed in freedom.

Despite the hardships, George was a brave and wise leader.

He rode on his horse he named Nelson, across the battlefields and inspired his troops with his determination and courage.

During the harsh winter at Valley Forge, George Washington and his soldiers faced great hardships; they were low on supplies, and many soldiers fell ill. But George never gave up - he led by example, staying with his troops, sharing their struggles, and working tirelessly to improve their conditions.

One night, when the soldiers were feeling discouraged, George went out into the snow and prayed. His faith gave him strength, and it also gave hope to the soldiers. They saw that their leader believed in their cause and that they were not alone.

With determination and strategic thinking, George led the Continental Army to many victories. He planned daring surprise attacks and outsmarted the British -

the major turning point came in 1781 at the Battle of Yorktown. With the help of French allies, George's army cornered the British, and after a fierce battle, they surrendered. After eight years, America won its freedom. The dream of an independent nation became real, and George, for his huge role in creating an independent nation became one of the founding fathers.

After the victory, people wanted George to become the first president of the United States.

Even though he had dreamed of retiring to his farm, he accepted the responsibility as he knew he had a critical role in shaping this new country.

As president, George made sure that the new government was fair and respected everyone's rights. He helped set up courts, chose the location for the White House, and established many traditions, like giving an inaugural address and the salutation 'Mr. President'.

George served two terms as president, from 1789-1797, 11 years after the USA had declared independence and then retired, setting the example that no leader should hold power forever.

When he wasn't being a general or president, George loved farming. He returned to his farm, Mount Vernon, where he spent his final years. He passed away on December 14, 1799, but his legacy lived on, with the capital city, Washington D.C. and the state of Washington, amongst other things named after him. In fact, he is on every one-dollar bill or quarter, so if you see him, take a moment to remember George and his journey from a mere farm boy to the founding father of the USA!

# John Adams

**Born:**
Oct 30, 1735

**Birthplace:**
Braintree, Massachussetts Bay

**Presidency:**
1797 - 1801

**Died:**
Jul 4, 1826

In the same era when George Washington was guiding America as its first president, there was another bright man preparing to shine - his name was John Adams.

John was born on October 30, 1735, in a small town in Massachusetts. His parents taught him the importance of working hard and being honest, and he certainly took those lessons to heart. He was such a good student that he went to Harvard University college when he was only sixteen years old! After graduating, John became a lawyer. But he didn't just argue cases; he was deeply involved in the politics of his time. As he grew older, John also began to dislike British rule and believed that the American colonies deserved to be independent, just like his friend George.

When the American Revolution started, John was chosen to represent Massachusetts in the Continental Congress, where leaders from all the colonies came together to make decisions. He was a persuasive speaker and played a major role in the decision to declare independence, making John Adams one of the founding fathers of the USA.

John helped write the Declaration of Independence and even suggested that his friend, Thomas Jefferson, write the first draft! He also served as a diplomat in Europe during the war, securing support and resources from other countries such as France, to help the colonies win their freedom.

John, with his background in law, would help shape the legal system in the USA too, creating a system of 'innocent until proven guilty' and a person's right to a lawyer when they have been accused of a crime.

After the war, John served as the first Vice President under George Washington. Then, in 1797, he was elected as the second President of the USA. He had big shoes to fill, but John was ready to work hard and do his best.

As President, John worked hard to keep his new nation at peace, and he succeeded - keeping America away from conflict from the UK and France while the Napoleonic Wars in Europe had begun.

It wasn't an easy decision, but John believed it was the best thing for the young country and this decision helped a young America retain its important allies and kept it out of a costly war.

John served one term as president and lost the second election in 1800 to Thomas Jefferson.

He went back to Massachusetts, where he spent his days writing and farming. He passed away on July 4, 1826 - exactly 50 years after the Declaration of Independence was adopted!

John was a man of strong beliefs, deep intelligence, and strong commitment to his country. John and his son, John Quincy Adams were the only presidents from the first twelve to not own any slaves.

# Thomas Jefferson

**Born:**
Apr 13, 1743

**Birthplace:**
Shadwell,
Virginia

**Presidency:**
1801 - 1809

**Died:**
Jul 4, 1826

Long ago, in the rolling hills of Virginia, a child named Thomas Jefferson was born on April 13, 1743. He loved to read, explore nature, and play the violin. Little did he know that he would one day grow up to become the third President of the United States!

Thomas was a brilliant student; he studied at the College of William and Mary and then became a lawyer - but his hunger for knowledge did not stop there. He studied everything from architecture to science, from philosophy to languages. In fact, Thomas was multilingual and could read and write in several languages, including Latin and Greek amongst others!

Thomas's life took a dramatic turn when he decided to join the fight for America's freedom. His contributions would secure him as one of the USA's founding fathers.

He was chosen to represent Virginia in the Continental Congress, where he met fellow patriots like John Adams and Benjamin Franklin who wanted independence. One year into the Revolutionary war against Great Britain, America would decide to declare its independence, and several key people would ask the previous president John Adams to write it. John would instead request that the much younger Thomas write it, because of his amazing talents. Congress would look at Thomas, and he agreed. Thomas would travel to a friend's house in Philadelphia, where for 17 days, in almost total isolation, Thomas would write the declaration. He worked day and night, writing with passion and clarity and laying the foundation for an independent nation.

Aged just 33 at the time, a young age for such a responsibility, Thomas completed his work, and presented it to Congress on June 28. The words were powerful, and several well known quotes such as "We hold these truths to be self-evident, that all men are created equal, that they are endowed by their creator with certain unalienable rights, that among these are life, liberty and the pursuit of happiness" became the chant for a new nation and still inspire us today.

Congress read it, making only a few changes since Thomas' writing was so skilled, ratified it on July 4th 1776.

This meant that they declared the USA an independent nation it to the public, and marking July 4th a day to be celebrated every year in the USA as independence day.

This of course meant that Britain no longer had control of the USA but they were not happy about this, so the Revolutionary War continued until 1783.

When it was over and America secured their victory, Thomas served as the American Minister to France, a country who helped the USA secure their independence, then as the Secretary of State under President George Washington, and then Vice President under John Adams.

In 1801, Thomas became the third President of the United States. During his presidency, he achieved many things, like purchasing the Louisiana Territory from France. This doubled the size of the USA, giving us the lands that would eventually become 15 new states, including Illinois, Ohio, Louisiana, Michigan and many more.

Soon after this purchase, two brave leaders and their men set out to explore these newly purchased lands in what was commonly known as the Lewis & Clark expedition.

Thomas also had a vision for education and believed in the importance of higher learning.
As a result, he founded the University of Virginia, which was the first university in the United States to be established on the principle of religious freedom. With his knowledge of architecture, Thomas designed the campus himself, and his contributions to education are still celebrated today.
Even after his presidency, he kept contributing to his nation.
Thomas Jefferson passed away from old age on July 4, 1826 - the same day as his friend and fellow founding father John Adams and exactly 50 years after the Declaration of Independence was signed! A big coincidence that is!
The story of Thomas Jefferson is a tale of a man with a love for learning, a passion for freedom, and a deep commitment to his country. His life teaches us the power of words and the importance of continual learning.

# James Madison

**Born:**
Apr 13, 1751

**Birthplace:**
Port Conway,
Virginia

**Presidency:**
1809 - 1817

**Died:**
Jun 28, 1836

Long ago, in the peaceful countryside of Virginia, a child named James Madison was born on March 16, 1751. From a young age, James had a curious mind. He loved to read and learn about everything he could. He was especially interested in the ways that people could work together to create a fair government.

James was a very good student, and when he grew up, he went to the College of New Jersey, which we now know as Princeton University. He studied so hard that he finished his studies in just two years!

When he returned to Virginia, James became involved in politics. He believed that the American colonies should be free from British rule. So, when the American Revolution began, he was ready to help lead the way.

James was elected to the Continental Congress, where he worked with other leaders like George Washington and Thomas Jefferson, but was only in his 20's during the Revolutionary war, so he didn't have a leading role like the previous presidents did.

He was quiet and small in stature and would have not been a great soldier, but his ideas were big and influential. He was dissatisfied with the current rules of the newly formed United States and the lack of organization in government. James worked tirelessly to address this, with the hopes to build a stronger foundation to build a great nation. He read countless books, attended meetings, and had long conversations with other brilliant minds. He wanted to make sure that this Constitution was fair, that it would allow each state to have a say, and that it would protect the rights of all people, not just the ones with the most power or money.

After months and months of hard work, and countless quills used up, James, along with a group of dedicated people, had done it. They had written the U.S. Constitution. It was a thing of beauty, with its elegant phrases and empowering ideas. It talked about the "We the People," and it set the rules for how the USA would be governed.

It was the first time such a document had been created, and people all around the world admired it.

It was such a splendid piece of work that James Madison became known as the "Father of the Constitution." The Constitution wasn't perfect, and it wasn't complete. It needed some changes and additions, so James helped write those too. These changes are called 'amendments', since these changes amended the original rules, and the first ten of them together are known as the Bill of Rights. These amendments made sure that people's basic rights, like freedom of speech and the right to a fair trial, were protected, the foundations of a thriving nation.

His massive contribution to the United States constitution, a document that shapes how our country is governed even today, earned the nickname "Father of the Constitution".

James also co-wrote the Federalist Papers, a series of essays that explained the Constitution and convinced people to support it. And he was a leading voice in creating the Bill of Rights, the first ten amendments to the Constitution that protect our freedoms, like freedom of speech and religion.

In 1809, James was elected as the fourth President of the United States.
His presidency was dominated by the War of 1812 against Britain. The war was difficult, bearing large losses of life and destruction for both the USA and the British. During the war, the British burnt down the White House, and the Capitol as retaliation for the USA's of British Canada. Despite this, the USA, under James' leadership, stayed strong and eventually made a truce with the British.
The result solidified the USA as an independent nation, away from British rule.
After serving two terms as President, James retired to his Virginia plantation, Montpelier, with his wife Dolley.
He spent his final years studying, writing, and farming.
James Madison passed away on June 28, 1836, but his legacy lives on. From the Constitution to the Bill of Rights, his ideas have helped shape our country and protect our freedoms. His name is honored in many ways, notably having the Madison Square Gardens in New York named after him.

# James Monroe

**Born:**
Apr 28, 1758

**Birthplace:**
Port Conway, Virginia

**Presidency:**
1817 - 1825

**Died:**
Jul 4, 1831

In the vibrant colony of Virginia, on April 28, 1758, a boy named James Monroe was born. His family wasn't wealthy, but they worked hard and taught James the value of persistence and dedication. Little did they know, their young son would grow up to become the fifth President of the United States!

As a teenager, James went to the College of William and Mary. But his studies were interrupted when the American Revolution broke out. Like many brave young men of his time, James left school to join the fight for freedom. He even crossed the Delaware River with George Washington in a famous surprise attack! In another battle, James suffered a severe injury while serving as an officer in the Continental Army.

He was struck in the shoulder by a musket ball during the Battle of Trenton in 1776. Remarkably, the bullet lodged itself in his shoulder, and he carried it for the rest of his life.

After the war, James studied law with Thomas Jefferson, their friendship starting during the Revolutionary war and began his journey in politics.

He was elected to the Virginia House of Delegates, then to the Congress under the Articles of Confederation. He served as a diplomat to France and as Secretary of State and Secretary of War under President James Madison.

In 1817, James was elected as the fifth President of the United States. His presidency is often called the "Era of Good Feelings" because it was a time of peace and national growth. As President, James would go on a groundbreaking tour of the country known as the "Goodwill Tour" or "Monroe's Tour." Starting in 1817, he embarked on a journey that covered over 15,000 miles and lasted over a year. This tour made him the first president to travel extensively throughout the United States and interact directly with the American people, a common thing for presidents today.

It wasn't all smooth sailing, though as there were still big debates about slavery and the balance of power between different parts of the country.

One of the most famous moments of his presidency was the Monroe Doctrine. This was a policy that said European countries shouldn't interfere in the Americas anymore. This was a big step in establishing the United States as its own independent country with their own rules and not just constantly pushed around by European countries, as James had witnessed during the 1812 war with Britain.

James served two terms as President. After that, he retired to his estate in Virginia, called Oak Hill. He passed away on July 4, 1831, becoming the third president (of five so far) to die on Independence Day!

For his contributions to laying foundations for the USA to become a great nation, he is a founding father, and the last president to be so.

# John Quincy Adams

**Born:**
Jul 11, 1767

**Birthplace:**
Braintree, Massachussetts Bay

**Presidency:**
1825 - 1829

**Died:**
Feb 23, 1848

In a small town in Massachusetts, on July 11, 1767, a man named John was born. He had quite the legacy to live up to - his father was none other than John Adams, the second President of the United States. As he grew up, John Quincy proved that he had his own contributions to make to history.

From a young age, John Quincy was exposed to the world of politics and diplomacy. He traveled with his father to Europe and learned about different cultures and languages. He was such a good student that he even served as an interpreter for his father! John was also a great swimmer and loved to swim when he got the opportunity.

When he grew up, John Quincy followed in his father's footsteps and became a diplomat, then a senator, and then Secretary of State under President James Monroe.

As Secretary of State, he helped create the Monroe Doctrine, which told European countries to leave the new nations in the Americas alone.

In 1825, John Quincy was elected as the sixth President of the United States. His election was unique because it was decided by the House of Representatives, not the usual electoral vote. This was because none of the four candidates received a majority of electoral votes.

While serving as President, John Quincy Adams received an unusual gift from Marquis de Lafayette, the French aristocrat and military officer who fought alongside the Americans during the Revolutionary War. Lafayette sent Adams an alligator as a pet. It was housed in the White House's East Room bathroom for several months before being transferred to a zoo.

John Quincy was a strong advocate for education, infrastructure, and scientific research. However, he faced opposition in Congress, which made it hard for him to get things done. After serving one term as President, he was defeated in his re-election bid.

John Quincy didn't retire from public life though, he continued his career in politics.

He was elected to the House of Representatives, where he served for seventeen years. This is where people from different states in the USA come together to represent the interests of the people within different states and create new laws.

He was a powerful voice against slavery and fought for the right of people to petition the government. He served in Congress until he passed away in 1848. John would write everyday, and his writings that span 70 years of his life give a valuable insight into U.S. history.

So that's the story of John Quincy Adams - a lifelong public servant who never stopped fighting for what he believed in. He taught us that even when things get tough, it's important to keep going and to keep standing up for what's right.

# Andrew Jackson

**Born:**
Mar 15, 1767

**Birthplace:**
Waxhaw Settlement, Carolina

**Presidency:**
1829 - 1837

**Died:**
Jun 8, 1845

A long time ago, on March 15, 1767, in a small log cabin on the border between North and South Carolina, a boy named Andrew Jackson was born. Growing up in the wild frontier, he learned about courage and resilience, traits that would shape his future in ways he could hardly imagine.
Andrew didn't have an easy childhood. He lost his parents at a young age and had to fend for himself. But that didn't stop him. He worked hard, studied law, and became a successful lawyer in Tennessee.
But Andrew was destined for more than just the law. He was a natural leader, and although has no military training, he was a brave soldier. During the War of 1812, he led American forces to a famous victory in the Battle of New Orleans against the British.

This was a very important city because it was a port, which meant it was a place where ships could come in and out, bringing goods and people. If Britain could capture New Orleans, they could control a big part of America's trade.

But Andrew Jackson and his brave soldiers were there to protect it. Despite the odds, Jackson's soldiers fought heroically against the British.

The British had more soldiers and better weapons, but Jackson and his men did not back down. They fought with courage and determination, and in the end, they won! The Battle of New Orleans was a decisive victory for America, and Andrew Jackson became a national hero. For his stern leadership and refusal to give up, Andrew would earn the nickname "Old Hickory" because his men said he was as tough as a hickory tree!

Andrew's military success propelled him into politics. He served as a congressman, a senator, and a military governor. In 1828, he was elected as the seventh President of the United States.

As President, Andrew was known for his fiery temper and strong will. He believed in the power of the common people and fought against what he saw as corruption and privilege amongst the rich.

This made him quite popular among many Americans, but some of his policies also led to controversy.

One of the most debated actions of his presidency was the Indian Removal Act, which led to the forced relocation of Native American tribes from their ancestral lands, known as the Trail of Tears. While some saw it as necessary for the nation's expansion, many others criticized it for its harshness and injustice.

Andrew also famously had a beloved pet parrot named Poll. The parrot was known for its colorful language and ability to imitate Jackson's swearing. It was said that Poll would often disrupt White House events with its loud and sometimes inappropriate squawks.

Andrew served two terms as President and then retired to his plantation in Tennessee, called the Hermitage. He passed away on June 8, 1845.

His legacy lives on, most famously with his face on the $20 bill, reminding us of his story and his determination to fight for the common American people.

# Martin Van Buren

**Born:**
Dec 5, 1782

**Birthplace:**
Kinderhook, New York

**Presidency:**
1837 - 1841

**Died:**
Jul 24, 1862

Many years ago, on December 5, 1782, in the quiet village of Kinderhook, New York State, a boy named Martin Van Buren was born. His father was a farmer and tavern owner, and Martin grew up in a bustling, diverse environment.

Martin was a very smart boy. Even though his family wasn't wealthy, he managed to study law and became a lawyer. He had a gift for speaking and politics, and he used these talents to serve his community and his country.

Before long, Martin was elected to the New York State Senate, then to the United States Senate. He served as Governor of New York, Secretary of State under President Andrew Jackson, and even as Vice President.

Clearly, Martin was moving up in the world of politics!

In 1836, Martin was elected as the President of the United States, making him the first president who was born after America declared its independence. He was also the first President whose parents were not born in America - his parents were Dutch! In fact, Martin's mother tongue is Dutch, and is the only president to use English was his second language, which he was fluent at!
During his presidency, Martin faced several challenges, like an economic crisis known as the Panic of 1837. He worked hard to guide the country through these tough times, although unfortunately, not many agreed with his policies.
Martin served one term as President and then continued to stay involved in politics. He even ran for President two more times, but he was not re-elected.
In his later years, Martin retired to his estate in Kinderhook, which he called Lindenwald. He passed away on July 24, 1862, leaving behind a legacy inspiring non-native English speakers (and native) that with hard work, anything is possible.

# William Henry Harrison

**Born:**
Feb 9, 1773

**Birthplace:**
Charles City County, Virginia

**Presidency:**
1841 (31 days)

**Died:**
Apr 4, 1841

on February 9, 1773, a boy named William was born on a plantation in Virginia. Little did he know that he would grow up to be a military hero and the ninth President of the United States!

As a young man, William went to college to study medicine, but when his father passed away, he couldn't afford to stay in school. So, he joined the army and headed to the wild frontier. There, he proved to be a brave soldier and an excellent leader.

One of William's most famous battles was the Battle of Tippecanoe. He and his troops fought against a confederation of Native American tribes. The battle was fierce, but in the end, William's forces were victorious. After this, people started calling him "Old Tippecanoe."

William served as the governor of the Indiana Territory for many years, where he continued to deal with frontier issues and conflicts. He also served as a congressman and a senator representing Ohio.

In 1840, William was elected as the ninth President of the United States. His campaign was unlike any other. His supporters used a log cabin as a symbol of his frontier toughness, even though William was born into a wealthy family. They even created a catchy campaign slogan, "Tippecanoe and Tyler Too," referring to William and his vice presidential running mate, John Tyler.

Unfortunately, William's presidency was cut tragically short. He gave a very long inaugural speech on a cold, wet day and fell ill with pneumonia. He passed away on April 4, 1841, just one month after becoming President, serving the shortest term of any American president.

Even though his presidency was short, the story of William Henry Harrison reminds us of the importance of resilience and dedication. From his bravery on the frontier to his dedication to public service, he left a mark on American history.

# John Tyler

**Born:**
Mar 29, 1790

**Birthplace:**
Greenway Plantation, Virginia

**Presidency:**
1841 - 1845

**Died:**
Jan 18, 1862

Long ago, in 1790, a boy named John was born in a small town in Virginia. He grew up on a plantation, surrounded by green fields and dense woods. Little did he know, he was destined to become the tenth President of the United States!

John was an excellent student and he loved to read and learn. When he grew up, he studied law and became a successful lawyer. Even with a great job, his ambitions didn't stop there. He had a passion for public service and was soon elected to the Virginia legislature.

John was a man of many talents. He served as a U.S. congressman, governor of Virginia, and U.S. senator. Then, in 1840, he was chosen as William Henry Harrison's running mate in the presidential election.

They had a catchy slogan, "Tippecanoe and Tyler Too," and they won the election.

But just one month after becoming Vice President, something unexpected happened. President Harrison fell ill and passed away. Suddenly, John Tyler was President of the United States. He was the first Vice President to become President due to the death of his predecessor.

John's presidency had many challenges. He had disagreements with his political party, the Whigs, and he faced issues like state rights and the expansion of slavery. Despite these challenges, John accomplished a lot, like bringing the state of Texas from Mexico into the Union, making it part of the USA.

After serving one term as President, John retired to his Virginia plantation, Sherwood Forest. He would go on to have a total of 15 children, a record for a president!

However, John wasn't done serving his country. When the Civil War broke out, he worked hard to try to keep the peace, though he eventually sided with the Confederacy. He passed away on January 18, 1862.

# James K. Polk

**Born:**
Nov 2, 1795

**Birthplace:**
Pineville,
North Carolina

**Presidency:**
1845 - 1849

**Died:**
Jun 15, 1849

Once upon a time, in a log cabin in North Carolina in 1795, a boy named James was born. Despite his humble beginnings, James was destined for big things.

James was a hard worker, even as a boy. He helped his family on the farm and worked hard in school. Like many of the presidents before him, he had a burning desire to gain knowledge and went on to study law. Soon after, he would become a successful lawyer and take up a hobby for politics.

Before long, James was elected to the Tennessee legislature and then to the U.S. House of Representatives, where he earned the nickname "Young Hickory" because his politics were similar to Andrew Jackson's, who was known as "Old Hickory."

James didn't stop there. He served as the Speaker of the House and the governor of Tennessee. Then, in 1844, he was elected as the President of the United States. He was the first dark horse, or unexpected, presidential nominee in U.S. history!

As President, James accomplished a lot. He led the country during the Mexican-American War, which the U.S. won, resulting in the addition of a lot of land. The land included states such as modern-day California, Nevada, Utah, Arizona and more. He settled the border with British Canada on the northern side too. The rapid expansion of the U.S. led to large increases in wealth for the country, thanks to the gold rush. When California became part of the USA, gold was found in 1848 and lots and lots of people began migrating from the east of the USA to the west, in search for riches. The California gold rush of 1848-1855 began an era that was commonly known as the Wild West!

James also established the Naval Academy and the Department of Interior. James was known for working tirelessly. He even fulfilled all of his campaign promises in just one term, more than what most other presidents had managed to accomplish in the same timeframe!

But being President is hard work, and after one term, James decided not to run for re-election.

He retired to his home in Tennessee, where he enjoyed a peaceful life until he passed away on June 15, 1849.

So, that's the story of James K. Polk, the eleventh President of the United States. His life shows us that with hard work and dedication, we can achieve great things. James rose from a log cabin to the White House, expanding the country and fulfilling his promises to the American people.

# Zachary Taylor

**Born:**
Nov 24, 1784

**Birthplace:**
Barboursville, Virginia

**Presidency:**
1849 - 1850

**Died:**
Jul 9, 1850

Zachary Taylor was born on November 24, 1784, in a modest home in Virginia. His family could not have known then that he would grow up to become a military hero and the twelfth President of the United States! Growing up, Zachary didn't go to school much, but he loved the great outdoors. As a young man, he chose a life of adventure and joined the army. He was very brave and became a respected military leader, earning him the nickname "Old Rough and Ready." Zachary fought in many battles, but he was most famous for his leadership during the Mexican-American War. His bravery and skill in this war helped the USA win the war, along with so much new territory and riches thanks to the Gold Rush, and therefore made him a national hero. In the eyes of the people, Zachary would be a great president..

And so Zachary did just that.

In 1848, Zachary was elected as the twelfth President of the United States. He wasn't a typical politician as had never voted in an election before becoming President! But because he was very popular, a hero and also a reputation for being honest and straightforward, this did not matter.

As President, the biggest issue Zachary faced was the question of whether new states should allow slavery. Zachary was a slave owner himself and wanted to keep the country united, so he worked towards compromises that might avoid a civil war.

The north, known as the Union wanted to abolish slavery across the whole USA, but the south, later called the confederacy, relied on slavery to make money, since the south mainly produced crops that needed slaves to be profitable, and this was understandably a difficult problem to solve peacefully.

Tragically, Zachary's time as President was cut short. He fell ill after a Fourth of July celebration in 1850 and passed away just a few days later. His term as President lasted only 16 months, and Zachary is still best known today as a national hero in the Mexican-American war.

# Millard Fillmore

**Born:**
Jan 7, 1800

**Birthplace:**
Moravia,
New York

**Presidency:**
1850 - 1853

**Died:**
Mar 8, 1870

Millard Fillmore was born on January 7, 1800, in a log cabin in the backwoods of New York.

As a child, Millard worked hard to help his family on their farm. He didn't have a lot of opportunities for schooling, but he loved to read. He taught himself many things and later worked his way through law school to become a lawyer. Despite not being wealthy yet, he made numerous donations of libraries, enriching them with books that could help educate others.

Millard's hard work and dedication soon led him into politics. He served in the New York State Assembly and the United States House of Representatives. Then, in 1848, he was chosen as Zachary Taylor's vice president in the presidential election, which they won!

But, of course something tragic would happen - Zachary's early death.

Suddenly, Millard was the President of the United States! He was the last president who was neither a Democrat nor a Republican - he was a member of the Whig Party.

As President, Millard was immediately plunged into the ongoing debate over slavery in the new western territories. Should California, or Texas, or Missouri be slave states or free states? The problem was the status of the states that lied on the border between north and south.

He tried to keep the peace by supporting the Compromise of 1850, which made concessions to both sides. This compromise involved declaring one state on the border a slave state, and another state on the border a free state, and was controversial and faced criticism from both the North and the South. The South thought that it was not enough of a concession, and the North thought Millard was not going far enough.

After serving out the rest of Taylor's term, Millard was not nominated by his party for a second term. But he remained active in public life, even helping to found the University of Buffalo.

Millard Fillmore passed away on March 8, 1874.

# Franklin Pierce

**Born:**
Nov 23, 1804

**Birthplace:**
Hillsborough, New Hampshire

**Presidency:**
1853 - 1857

**Died:**
Oct 8, 1869

On November 23, 1804, a boy named Franklin Pierce was born in a little log cabin in New Hampshire.

Franklin was a charming boy who grew up to be a hard-working young man. He went to school at Bowdoin College where he met a lifelong friend, the famous writer Nathaniel Hawthorne. After college, Franklin studied law and became a lawyer, but his journey didn't stop there. He felt called to serve his community and soon entered politics. Franklin served in the New Hampshire legislature and then in the U.S. House of Representatives. Later, he became a U.S. senator. During the Mexican-American War, he served as a brigadier general, showing his bravery and leadership.

In 1852, Franklin was nominated as the Democratic candidate for President. He wasn't the most well-known candidate, but he was well-liked and had a reputation for being honest. He won the election and became the fourteenth President of the United States!

Franklin's presidency was dominated by similar issues to his predecessor; trying to address the tension between the North and the South over slavery. Franklin tried to maintain peace and unity, but like Millard, his efforts were often not successful, and the USA slipped ever closer towards a civil war.

After serving one term as President, Franklin returned to his home in New Hampshire. His personal life was very sad in his post-presidency years. Initially having three children, two sons had died due to illnesses and then his wife and last son had died due to a collision with a train. He was very sad at his losses and struggled to cope. He passed away on October 8, 1869.

# James Buchanan

**Born:**
Apr 23, 1791

**Birthplace:**
Cove Gap, Pennsylvania

**Presidency:**
1857 - 1861

**Died:**
Jun 1, 1868

James Buchanan was born in 1791, in a small town in Pennsylvania.

As a young man, James was very ambitious. He studied law and became a successful lawyer. But his ambitions didn't stop there. He felt the pull towards politics and public service, and he was soon elected to the Pennsylvania legislature.

James proved to be a dedicated public servant. He served in the U.S. House of Representatives, as U.S. minister to Russia, and as Secretary of State. He also served as the U.S. minister to the United Kingdom, where he helped draft the Ostend Manifesto, a controversial document suggesting the U.S. should acquire Cuba from Spain.

In 1856, James was elected as the fifteenth President of the United States. He was the only president to be a bachelor, meaning that he was not married, and his niece, Harriet Lane, acted as First Lady during his presidency.

James's presidency biggest issue was again the growing divide between the North and South over slavery. James struggled to maintain peace and unity, favoring a policy that unfortunately did not do enough to prevent the looming Civil War between the two sides.

After serving one term, James retired to his estate in Pennsylvania, known as Wheatland. He watched from the sidelines as the nation he had once led was plunged into a brutal civil war. He passed away on June 1, 1868.

# Abraham Lincoln

**Born:**
Feb 12, 1809

**Birthplace:**
Sinking Spring Farm, Kentucky

**Presidency:**
1861 - 1865

**Died:**
Jun 1, 1865

Abraham Lincoln was born on February 12th, 1809 in a little log cabin in Kentucky.

His parents, Thomas and Nancy, were poor but hard-working folks who taught young Abe the value of honesty and hard work. This humble beginning would shape the character of a man destined to be one of America's greatest presidents.

Growing up, Abraham loved to read. He borrowed books from his neighbors and read by the light of the fireplace, eager to learn as much as he could. He wasn't just a bookworm, though. He was strong and tall, often helping his father chop wood for the fire.

When Abraham was just nine, his mother, Nancy, fell sick and died. It was a tough time for the little boy.

However, he found comfort in his new stepmother, Sarah, who encouraged his love for reading and learning. She recognized something special in him and believed he was meant for great things.

In his early twenties, Abraham moved to Illinois, where he worked a variety of jobs. He split logs, managed a store, and even captained a riverboat, where he invented a device that would lift boats over obstructions in the river - he would manage to get a patent for this invention, but it was never manufactured or sold. He would also take up wrestling, where he only lost one out of nearly 300 matches, earning him the reputation of an exceptional wrestler in his community.

But Abraham never forgot his love for books and ideas. He began to study law and started participating in local politics.

As he grew older, Abraham became a lawyer and a successful politician, known for his honesty and integrity. That's why people started to call him 'Honest Abe.' He could tell a great story, make people laugh, and most importantly, he always stood up for what he believed was right.

In 1860, Honest Abe was elected as the 16th president of the United States. It was a difficult time.

The country was divided over many issues, especially slavery. Abe believed that all people, no matter their color, should be free. But not everyone agreed.

Just a few months after Abe became president, the Civil War began. It was a painful time, brother fighting against brother.

But President Lincoln stayed strong, leading his country through the most challenging time in its history.

In the middle of the war, in 1863, Lincoln signed the Emancipation Proclamation. This important document declared that all enslaved people in the rebellious states were free. It was a big step towards ending slavery in the entire country.

Later in 1863, after one of the bloodiest battles during the Civil War in Gettysburg, Abe travelled to Gettysburg to mourn the dead and to give what would become one of the most famous speeches of an American president, the Gettysburg Address.

For his speech, Abe stood tall in his big, black stovepipe hat and delivered a speech that was quite short but very powerful.

In his speech, he reminded everyone that America was a nation "conceived in Liberty, and dedicated to the proposition that all men are created equal."

These words referenced the Declaration of Independence, signed 87 years ago, and its promise of freedom and equality for all. He spoke of the bravery of the soldiers who had fought and urged the people to continue the fight for a "new birth of freedom," so that the government of the people, by the people, and for the people, "shall not perish from the earth."

Abraham Lincoln's words at Gettysburg remind us of the bravery and sacrifice of those who fought for freedom during the Civil War.

They also remind us of the values that America was built on and why it's important to continue the fight for equality and freedom for all.

The war finally ended in 1865, with Abe able to save the USA from falling apart into two separate countries.

However, only a few days later, President Lincoln was shot at a theatre and died. The whole nation mourned the loss of a great leader.

Although his life was cut short, Abraham Lincoln's legacy lives on. He's remembered as the president who preserved the USA and helped to end slavery. He showed us that no matter where we come from, with honesty, hard work, and a belief in justice, we can make a big difference.

# Andrew Johnson

**Born:**
Dec 29, 1808

**Birthplace:**
Raleigh,
North Carolina

**Presidency:**
1865 - 1869

**Died:**
Jul 31, 1875

In a tiny, wooden house in North Carolina, on a cold December day in 1808, Andrew Johnson was born. He didn't come from a wealthy family. In fact, his parents Jacob and Mary were very poor. They could not afford to send him to school, but that didn't stop Andrew from dreaming big.

When Andrew was still very young, his father passed away. To help support his family, he started working as a tailor's apprentice. Tailoring is a job that requires patience and attention to detail, and it was here that young Andrew learned the value of hard work and precision.

Although Andrew didn't go to school, he had an insatiable thirst for knowledge. His wife, Eliza, taught him how to read and write.

Every day, after a long day of stitching and mending, Andrew would read books by the candlelight, slowly teaching himself everything he'd missed out on in school.

Andrew's journey from a tailor to the world of politics started in Greeneville, Tennessee. He began by becoming the mayor of Greeneville and then a member of the Tennessee state legislature. People liked him because he understood and could relate to their struggles. He was a common man himself, after all!

Before long, Andrew climbed the ladder of success. He served as a congressman, governor, and even as a senator. Despite his humble beginnings, he made a name for himself in the world of politics with his dedication to the common people of the USA.

In 1864, during the height of the Civil War, President Abraham Lincoln chose Andrew to be his vice president, hoping to unite the North and the South. But just a few months later, Lincoln was tragically assassinated, and Andrew Johnson became president.

Andrew's time in office involved repairing a country that was still recovering from the Civil War, and many people disagreed about how to bring the Southern states back into the Union.

Johnson faced opposition from Congress, but he did his best to stitch the torn nation back together, just as he had stitched clothes as a young boy.

He passed laws to help poor Southerners, both white and black, and worked hard to rebuild the country. But it was a difficult task, and not everyone was happy with his leadership. He failed to give African Americans the rights the Emancipation Proclamation had promised, and he even survived an impeachment trial, a trial that sought to kick him out of the presidents role, becoming the first US President to do so!

# Ulysses S. Grant

**Born:**
Apr 27, 1822

**Birthplace:**
Point Pleasant, Ohio

**Presidency:**
1869 - 1877

**Died:**
Jul 23, 1885

In a cozy house in Ohio, on a spring day in April 1822, a child named Hiram Ulysses Grant was born. His parents, Jesse and Hannah, named him Hiram after his grandfather, but everyone just called him 'Ulysses.'

As a young boy, Ulysses was quiet and shy. He liked to spend time with horses, and he was really good at riding them. This skill would become handy later in his life.

When Ulysses was 17, his father sent him to a military school called West Point. There was a mix-up at the school, and they registered him as "Ulysses S. Grant," adding an 'S' for his mother's maiden name, Simpson.

He liked it and decided to keep it.

Ulysses graduated from West Point and served in the Mexican-American War.

After the war, he left the army to be with his beloved wife, Julia, and their children and worked in his father's leather goods store. But when the Civil War started in 1861, he felt it was his duty to help and abolish slavery, so he returned to the military.

Soon, Grant proved to be an excellent leader on the battlefield. His strategy and determination helped him win many battles. One of his first great victories was the capture of Fort Donelson in Tennessee. When the Confederate general asked for terms of surrender, Grant famously replied, "No terms except an unconditional and immediate surrender can be accepted." From then on, he was known as "Unconditional Surrender" Grant.

But perhaps the most famous battle Grant led was the Siege of Vicksburg. This was a very important battle because Vicksburg was a major stronghold for the Confederacy. After a long and difficult fight, Grant's army finally won, and this victory was a turning point in the Civil War. Because of his successes, President Abraham Lincoln promoted Grant to be the commander of all Union armies.

Grant was a tough but fair general; he pushed his troops hard, but he also cared for their welfare.

He understood that war was difficult and did his best to end the Civil War quickly.

In 1865, the Civil War finally came to an end when General Robert E. Lee of the Confederacy surrendered to Grant at Appomattox Court House in Virginia. Grant was generous in victory. He allowed the defeated soldiers to go home with their horses, knowing they would be needed for spring planting. This act of kindness helped to start healing the nation after such a long and painful war.

After the war, Grant's popularity led him to the White House. He was elected the 18th president of the United States in 1869. As president, he worked to ensure that the rights of all citizens, including newly freed African Americans, were protected. He believed in a peaceful and united nation where everyone could live freely.

But President Grant faced many challenges too. He had to deal with economic troubles and scandals in his administration. Despite these problems, he remained committed to his vision of a united, peaceful America.

After serving two terms as president, Ulysses S. Grant retired from public life.

# Rutherford B. Hayes

**Born:**
Oct 4, 1822

**Birthplace:**
Delaware,
Ohio

**Presidency:**
1877 - 1881

**Died:**
Jan 17, 1893

On October of 1822, in the state of Ohio, a child named Rutherford Birchard Hayes was born. His father had passed away before he was born, and his mother, Sophia, raised him with love and care. Little did anyone know that this boy would grow up to become the 19th President of the United States.

Rutherford, or "Rud" as his friends called him, loved to read. He was a good student and worked hard at school. His efforts led him to Kenyon College, and later, Harvard Law School, where he became a brilliant lawyer.

When the Civil War broke out, Rutherford felt it was his duty to help his country. So, he left his law practice and joined the Union Army.

Hayes wasn't just any soldier - he quickly rose through the ranks and became a Brigadier General, a high rank that showed he was a strong and capable leader. His men respected him, not just because he was their superior, but because he was fair, kind, and always put his soldiers' needs first.

One of the key battles Hayes fought in was the Battle of South Mountain in 1862. It was a fierce fight, but Hayes, even though he was injured, refused to leave the field until the battle was over. His courage inspired his men, and they fought bravely, helping the North win the battle. His bravery earned him the nickname "Rutherford the Brave."

After the war, Rutherford entered politics. He served as a congressman and then as the governor of Ohio, always fighting for equal rights for all, especially the newly freed slaves.

In 1876, Rutherford B. Hayes ran for president. The election was one of the closest in history, filled with tension and uncertainty. But in the end, Rutherford was declared the winner and became the president of the United States.

As president, he worked to heal the country's wounds from the Civil War.

He ended the era known as Reconstruction and brought the troops home from the South. He also started reforms in the government, aiming to make it less corrupt and more efficient.

Rutherford was known as a president of integrity and honesty. He made a promise to serve only one term, and he kept his word. After his term ended in 1881, he returned to Ohio with his wife, Lucy, the first First Lady to be called by that title.

In his post-presidency years, he continued to work for the causes he believed in, such as education for all and prison reform. His life of service didn't end with his presidency; it was a lifelong commitment. Rutherford would pass away in 1893 at age 70.

# James A. Garfield

**Born:**
Nov 19, 1831

**Birthplace:**
Moreland Hills
Ohio

**Presidency:**
1881

**Died:**
Sep 19, 1881

James Abram Garfield was born on a November day in 1831, in a log cabin in Ohio. \
His father, Abram, passed away when James was just a toddler, leaving his mother, Eliza, to raise him and his siblings alone. Times were hard, but this didn't stop James from dreaming big.

Young James loved to learn, he would often be found with his face in a book, reading by the firelight. He was a bright child and worked hard at school, and soon, he was ready for college. Even though he didn't have much money, James was determined to get an education. So, he worked as a carpenter and a teacher to pay for his studies.

James went to Williams College in Massachusetts and graduated with honors. He loved learning so much that he became a teacher, and later, a principal of a school.

He believed in the power of education to change lives.

When the Civil War began, James felt it was his duty to help his country. He joined the Union Army and showed great bravery and leadership. He fought in many battles and rose to the rank of Major General, just like the previous president, Rutherford.

After the war, James entered the world of politics. He served as a congressman for many years, always working hard for the people of Ohio. His honesty and dedication earned him the respect of his peers.

In 1880, James was nominated to run for president, and he won! He became the 20th president of the United States. President Garfield had big ambitions for his presidency. He wanted to improve education, modernize the Navy, and make sure everyone was treated fairly.

But sadly, his time in office was cut short. Just a few months after his inauguration, President Garfield was shot by a man named Charles Guiteau. He fought bravely for his life, but after 80 days, he passed away before he could put the plans he set forth to do into action.

# Chester A. Arthur

**Born:**
Oct 5, 1829

**Birthplace:**
Moreland Hills, Ohio

**Presidency:**
1881 - 1885

**Died:**
Nov 18, 1886

On a wet October day in 1829, in the small state of Vermont, a boy named Chester Alan Arthur was born. His father was a Baptist preacher, and his mother was a schoolteacher, and together, they raised Chester and his siblings with the values of hard work, honesty, and respect for all people.

Chester was a bright student who loved learning. After graduating from Union College in New York, he became a lawyer where he enjoyed spending many years fighting for people's rights and making sure the law was fair for everyone.

During the Civil War, Chester served as the Quartermaster General of New York. He was in charge of food, clothing, and supplies for the soldiers.

It was a big responsibility, and Chester made sure the soldiers had everything they needed.

After the war, Chester got involved in politics. He became the Collector of the Port of New York, a very important job that was basically like being the taxman for every ship that docked in New York. He was known for his honesty and fairness, which earned him the nickname 'The Gentleman Boss.'

In 1880, Chester was selected to be the Vice President to President James A. Garfield. But when President Garfield was tragically assassinated, Chester became the president.

As president, Chester surprised everyone. Even though he was known as 'The Gentleman Boss,' he didn't let his old friends take advantage of his new position. He worked hard to reform the government and make it less corrupt. He signed the Pendleton Act, a law that changed how government jobs were given, making it based on merit, not on who you knew.

Chester was known for his elegance and style. He loved hosting parties at the White House, which he had beautifully redecorated.

Chester served one term before suffering from poor health, where he sadly passed away just one year after his presidency.

# Grover Cleveland

**Born:**
Mar 5, 1837

**Birthplace:**
Caldwell,
New Jersey

**Presidency:**
1885 - 1889
1893 - 1897

**Died:**
Jun 24, 1908

Long ago, on a chilly March day in 1837 in New Jersey, a child named Stephen Grover Cleveland was born. He was the fifth of nine children, and his father was a humble minister.

Grover, as he preferred to be called, was not a rich child. He had to leave school at the age of 16 to help support his family. But Grover didn't let this stop him. He read a lot and taught himself what he couldn't learn in school.

Eventually, Grover moved to Buffalo, New York, where he worked as a lawyer. His honesty and hard work impressed everyone around him. He soon entered politics, first becoming the mayor of Buffalo and then the governor of New York.

In 1884, Grover was elected the 22nd president of the United States. He was the first Democrat to be elected after the Civil War. As president, Grover worked hard to make the government honest and efficient. He believed that the government should interfere as little as possible in people's lives.

After serving one term, he lost the next election to Benjamin Harrison. But Grover didn't give up, as he really enjoyed being president, and so following his heart, he ran again four years later, and guess what? He won!

He became the 24th president, after being the 22nd president, making him the only president in American history to serve two non-consecutive terms!

As the 24th president, Grover continued to work for the people. He handled difficult issues with courage and honesty. He also got married while he was president and had a baby girl, who was the first child to be born in the White House!

After his second term, Grover retired from politics. He spent his last years happily with his family in New Jersey.

# Benjamin Harrison

**Born:**
Aug 20, 1833

**Birthplace:**
Caldwell,
New Jersey

**Presidency:**
1889 - 1893

**Died:**
Mar 13, 1901

Benjamin Harrison was born a big farmhouse in Ohio, on a hot August day in 1833.

His grandfather, William Henry Harrison, was the 9th President of the United States. But nobody knew then that young Benjamin would follow in his grandfather's footsteps...

Benjamin was a studious child who loved reading and learning. He went to Miami University in Ohio, where he studied law.

After graduation, he moved to Indianapolis, Indiana, where he started his law practice and met his future wife, Caroline.

When the Civil War broke out, Benjamin felt it was his duty to serve his country. He joined the Union Army and fought bravely, rising to the rank of Brigadier General.

After the war, Benjamin returned to his law practice, but his leadership skills and passion for justice drew him into politics.

He served as a senator for Indiana before running for president.

In 1888, Benjamin was elected president. His victory was unique because he lost the popular vote but won the electoral vote. This means that while fewer people voted for him overall, he won in the states that had more electoral votes.

As president, Benjamin worked hard to modernize America; he helped pass the Sherman Antitrust Act, which was designed to stop big businesses from becoming too powerful. He also signed into law the McKinley Tariff and the Sherman Silver Purchase Act, both of which affected the country's economy.

Benjamin loved nature and wanted to protect it. He set aside more than 13 million acres of land as national forests, a legacy that we can still enjoy today. Benjamin's presidency also saw the addition of six new states to the Union: North Dakota, South Dakota, Montana, Washington, Idaho, and Wyoming.

After serving one term, Benjamin returned to his law practice. He also taught law at Stanford University and wrote a book about the government.

# William McKinley

**Born:**
Jan 29, 1843

**Birthplace:**
Niles,
Ohio

**Presidency:**
1897 - 1901

**Died:**
Sep 14, 1901

In a small house in Ohio, on a sunny day in January 1843, a boy named William McKinley was born. He was the seventh child in his family, and his parents would have no idea that their son would grow up to be president.

William was a thoughtful boy who loved to read. When he grew up, he became a school teacher. But when the Civil War broke out, he felt it was his duty to serve his country. At just age 18, he joined the Union Army as a private, but by the end of the war, he was a major!

After the war, William studied law and became a lawyer. He then entered the world of politics, serving in the U.S. House of Representatives and as governor of Ohio.

He always listened to the people and worked hard to make their lives better.

In 1896, William ran for president. His campaign was unique. Instead of traveling around the country, he spoke to people from his front porch in Ohio. Thousands of people came to hear him speak, and they liked what he had to say.

As president, William led America into a new century. He believed in the "gold standard," which made America's money more stable, and with this, he saw the economy of the country improve.

He also wanted to help Cuba gain independence and so asked Spain to let go of Cuba. When they refused, William declared war on Spain and led the country during the Spanish-American War, which resulted in a win for America and gaining control of the former Spanish colonies of Puerto Rico, Cuba Guam, and the Philippines. The USA would give Cuba their freedom a few years later.

In the same time period, the USA would invade Hawaii and make Hawaii part of the USA.

William was known as a kind and caring president. He once even saved his pet parrot from a fire in the White House!

William also had a connection to the world of American football.

He served as the honorary president of the Canton Bulldogs, a professional football team based in Canton, Ohio, during his presidency. The team would later become a founding member of the National Football League (NFL).

Sadly, William's presidency ended in tragedy when he was assassinated in 1901. But his legacy lives on. He was a president who cared deeply about his country and its people.

# Theodore Roosevelt

**Born:**
Oct 27, 1858

**Birthplace:**
New York City,
New York

**Presidency:**
1901 - 1909

**Died:**
Jan 6, 1919

Theodore Roosevelt was born in 1858, in the bustling city of New York. Everyone called him by his nickname "Teddy." Teddy was a sickly child, often battling his illnesses, but he never let this stop him. Instead, he believed that he could overcome anything with determination and grit.

As a young boy, Teddy loved reading about heroic explorers and mighty warriors. These stories inspired him to get stronger and overcome his illnesses. So, he began to exercise and push his body to the limits. Teddy also had a special love for animals and nature. He collected insects, watched birds, and studied the animals around him. His love for nature remained with him throughout his life.

When Teddy grew up, he went to Harvard University, where he did well in his studies and continued his physical training. After finishing school, he faced many challenges. He lost his beloved wife and mother on the same day, which left him heartbroken. To heal his sorrow, he moved to the wild western state of Dakota, where he learned to ride a horse, rope cattle, and live like a true cowboy. It was tough work, but Theodore didn't mind. He loved the challenge and the thrill of life on the open range.

When he returned to New York, Teddy entered politics. He held several positions, including being a police commissioner and the governor of New York. He was a man of action and believed in "the strenuous life," one of hard work, perseverance, and adventure.

In 1901, something extraordinary happened: Teddy became the President of the United States! He was the youngest person to ever become President. As President, Teddy was known for his energetic personality and his love for adventure. He was a strong leader who fought for the rights of workers and for fair business practices.

But do you remember Teddy's love for nature? Well, as President, he protected hundreds of millions of acres of land for national parks and forests.

Thanks to him, we can now enjoy places like the Grand Canyon and Yosemite National Park, some of the most well-known national parks in the USA.

He won the Nobel Peace Prize in 1906, making him the first American to win this prestigious award. Teddy was a true peacemaker, helping end a war between Russia and Japan.

After his presidency, Teddy continued to live life to the fullest. He went on an expedition to Africa, where he observed nature and collected specimens for the Smithsonian Institution. He also decided to venture to the unexplored areas of the Amazon Rainforest in South America.

Along with a team of explorers, he planned to chart the River of Doubt, a mysterious river hidden deep in the Amazon Rainforest. Nobody knew where it started or where it ended. It was a river shrouded in mystery, but that only made it more exciting for our adventurous Teddy!

As they sailed deeper into the heart of the rainforest, Theodore and his team faced dangers of all sorts. There were treacherous rapids that threatened to topple their canoes, and pesky insects that buzzed all around. Hungry piranhas swam in the water, and jaguars prowled in the shadows.

And of course, there was the relentless heat and the pouring rain.

Teddy kept a diary of his adventures and a lot of common knowledge of the Amazon came from Teddy's findings. For example, the stereotype of piranha's viciously eating flesh off a bone came from Teddy's observation of a group of hungry piranhas eating a cow alive in the water. This behavior is actually uncommon for piranhas.

Teddy ended up successfully navigating the River of Doubt and it was named Rio Roosevelt in his honor.

Teddy Roosevelt lived a full and exciting life, filled with adventure and purpose. He was a real-life hero, just like the ones he used to read about in his books. His courage, love for nature, and belief in justice still inspire us today. So, whenever you visit a beautiful national park or hear a story about a fearless leader, remember Teddy, the President who made it possible for us to enjoy these wonders.

The teddy bear was also named after Theodore, where the name originated from an incident during one of Roosevelt's hunting trips when he spared the life of a bear cub. This event inspired a political cartoon that led to the creation of the Teddy Bear.

# William Howard Taft

**Born:**
Sep 15, 1857

**Birthplace:**
Cincinnati
Ohio

**Presidency:**
1909 - 1913

**Died:**
Mar 8, 1930

Long ago, in the year 1857, a boy named William Howard Taft was born in the city of Cincinnati, Ohio. His friends and family would often call him "Will." Will was the son of a judge, and he grew up with a big family of five siblings!

From the beginning, Will was a bright boy who loved to learn. He was an excellent student and, just like his father, he had a deep interest in law and justice. When he grew up, he followed his father's footsteps and became a lawyer.

But Will didn't stop there. He was a man of many talents and ambitions. He served as a judge, the Governor of the Philippines, and even as Secretary of War. Imagine that! He went from a law office in Ohio to working in the White House!

Then, in 1908, something remarkable happened. Will was elected as the 27th President of the United States. His presidency was full of important decisions and actions. He worked hard to improve our country's legal system and helped make the government more efficient.

One of the unique things about President Taft is that he is the only person in history who has served as both President and Chief Justice of the United States Supreme Court. That's right! After his term as President, he was appointed as the Chief Justice, the highest position in the Supreme Court. This was actually his dream job, and he loved it even more than being President!

As President and Chief Justice, he made many decisions that still impact our country today. He always tried to be fair and make sure that everyone was treated equally under the law.

But life wasn't all about work for William Howard Taft. He loved to laugh and spend time with his family. He had a jolly personality, and he was also known for his size. In fact, he was so big that he got stuck in the White House bathtub! They had to get a special bathtub just for him.

# Woodrow Wilson

**Born:**
Dec 28, 1856

**Birthplace:**
Staunton
Virginia

**Presidency:**
1913 - 1921

**Died:**
Feb 3, 1924

In 1856, in the small town of Staunton, Virginia, a child named Thomas Woodrow Wilson was born. People often just called him "Woodrow." Born just before the Civil War, Woodrow grew up in a world that was changing quickly.

Woodrow was a curious and clever boy. But he faced a big challenge: learning was hard for him because he had dyslexia, a condition that makes reading and writing difficult. But Woodrow didn't let that stop him. He worked hard, and with the help of his father, he learned to love books and knowledge.

When Woodrow grew up, he went to Princeton University, then studied law, and even became a professor! He loved teaching and sharing his knowledge with others.

He wrote many books and eventually became the president of Princeton University.

But Woodrow's journey didn't stop there. He had a great interest in helping people and making the world a better place. This led him to politics, and he became the governor of New Jersey. He worked hard to make life better for the people in his state.

Then, in 1912, Woodrow was elected as the 28th President of the United States. Just a year into his presidency, the world would be plunged into difficult times. Two European countries, Austria and Serbia, declared war on each other, but because both these countries had allies, such as Russia, France, Germany and the UK, they got dragged into the war too, starting what was known as World War I. The war was the first global war and was more devastating than any war before it.

Woodrow believed in peace and wanted to find a way to end the war. He came up with a plan called the "Fourteen Points," which was his idea for peace and fairness among all countries.

Woodrow originally remained neutral during WW1, believing peace was the way, but after the fact that Germany tried to encourage Mexico to invade the USA, the USA finally declared war in 1917.

Germany surrendered 1 year later in 1918. He helped to create the League of Nations, an organization where countries could come together to talk about their problems instead of fighting and causing massive devastation as WW1 did. For his efforts to bring peace, Woodrow was awarded the Nobel Peace Prize. He was the second American president to receive this honor.

Unfortunately, as the war came to an end, another global issue began, the 1918 Spanish Flu, which proved to be a tough time for Woodrow and the USA. Despite Woodrow's best efforts to protect people from the flu, it became one of the deadliest pandemics.

Outside of work, Woodrow was an avid baseball fan. During his presidency, he frequently attended baseball games and even played catch on the White House lawn with his son and the Washington Senators baseball team.

However, being president was a tough job, and the stress took a toll on Woodrow's health. In his second term, he suffered a severe stroke, but he kept working as much as he could until his term ended.

Woodrow Wilson was a dedicated teacher, a thoughtful leader, and a peacemaker. He had a big dream for a world where countries would work together in peace.

# Warren G. Harding

**Born:**
Nov 2, 1865

**Birthplace:**
Blooming Grove
Ohio

**Presidency:**
1921 - 1923

**Died:**
Aug 2, 1923

Warren Gamaliel Harding was born in a small town in Ohio called Corsica in 1865. Warren, or "Winnie" as his family called him, grew up in a big family with seven siblings!

As a young boy, Warren loved to read newspapers as his parents owned a local newspaper company, and he learned to help with all parts of the process, from writing to printing. This sparked a love for journalism, and he carried this passion into adulthood. Eventually, he became the owner of a newspaper himself, called 'The Marion Star.'

Warren was a friendly and charming person, always ready to lend an ear or give a helping hand.

He was well-liked in his community, and these qualities helped him when he decided to enter politics. He served as an Ohio state senator and then as a U.S. senator. Then, in the year 1920, Warren won the people's vote and became the 29th President of the United States. Moving past World War 1, his campaign slogan was "Return to Normalcy," which meant he wanted to help America return to how it was before the war. As President, Warren worked hard to make America a peaceful, prosperous place. He supported new laws to protect children's rights and limit the work hours for railroad workers. He also supported women's rights and was the first President to have women in his cabinet.

Warren was known for his love of golf and poker, and he liked to keep a relaxed and friendly atmosphere in the White House. He was also the first President to have a speech broadcasted on the radio.

Sadly, Warren's time as President was cut short when in 1923, while in San Francisco, he suddenly fell ill and passed away.

After his death, several scandals involving Warren surfaced, most famously the teapot dome, where his government accepted bribes to give government-owned oil wells to certain oil companies, tarnishing his good reputation.

# Calvin Coolidge

**Born:**
Jul 4, 1872

**Birthplace:**
Plymouth Notch
Vermont

**Presidency:**
1923 - 1929

**Died:**
Jan 5, 1933

Once upon a time, in the small rural town of Plymouth Notch, Vermont, in 1872, a boy named John Calvin Coolidge Jr. was born. Known as "Cal," he was a quiet and thoughtful child who grew up surrounded by the simple beauties of the countryside.

Cal's family taught him the values of hard work, honesty, and responsibility from an early age. His father was a farmer and a storekeeper, and he also held various local government positions. Cal would often help his father with chores, developing a strong work ethic that would guide him throughout his life.

Cal was an excellent student who loved to read. He went to Amherst College in Massachusetts, where he studied hard and proved to be a great debater.

After graduating, he became a lawyer, and just like his father, he also got involved in local government.

Cal's honesty, dedication, and quiet strength made him well-liked, and he rose in politics, serving as a city solicitor, a state senator, and then the governor of Massachusetts.

In 1920, Cal's life took a remarkable turn when he was elected as Vice President of the United States alongside President Warren G. Harding. But just a few years later, President Harding suddenly passed away, and Cal became the 30th President of the United States.

Cal was known as a man of few words, earning him the nickname "Silent Cal." But don't be fooled! Even though he was quiet, he was a strong and effective leader. He believed in small government, individual responsibility, and the importance of business for the prosperity of America.

One of the most significant things about President Coolidge was that he was the first President to have his inauguration broadcasted on the radio. This allowed people all across the country to hear his voice and feel connected to the event, even if they couldn't be there in person.

Despite being a quiet man, Cal had a quirky side too!

He had a pet raccoon named Rebecca who lived in the White House. Rebecca was often seen roaming the grounds and occasionally joined the family at the dinner table. On top of the raccoon, Calvin loved animals and kept dogs, cats, canaries and even a bobcat in the White House.

After serving as President, Cal returned to his quiet life in Northampton, Massachusetts. He wrote a memoir, gave speeches, and enjoyed simple pleasures like reading and fishing.

Calvin Coolidge, the quiet boy from Vermont, left a significant mark on America with his firm, principled leadership.

# Herbert Hoover

**Born:**
Aug 10, 1874

**Birthplace:**
West Branch
Iowa

**Presidency:**
1929 - 1933

**Died:**
Oct 20, 1964

In the year 1874, in a small town of West Branch, Iowa, a boy named Herbert Clark Hoover was born. Herbert, or "Bert" as he was often called, was the first president born west of the Mississippi River.

Bert had a difficult childhood. Both of his parents died when he was very young, so he and his siblings lived with different relatives. These tough times didn't stop Bert, though. He was a determined boy and always believed that with hard work and honesty, you could overcome any challenge.

Bert was an excellent student, especially in math and science. He studied hard and became the first student from his town to attend Stanford University in California.

After he finished school, he became a successful mining engineer, traveling to far-off places like Australia and China for his work. This is a departure from conventional jobs such as a lawyer that prior presidents normally held.

Bert was always eager to help others. During World War I, he led efforts to get food to people in need in Europe, earning him the nickname "The Great Humanitarian." He believed that everyone should have enough to eat, no matter where they lived or what their situation was.

In 1928, Bert's hard work, intelligence, and caring nature led him to the highest office in the land - he became the 31st President of the United States. He was a brilliant man, and as president, he wanted to help all Americans live better lives.

However, just a few months after he became President, the United States faced a huge challenge. The Great Depression began, which was a time when many people lost their jobs, and there wasn't enough money or food for everyone. Times were so bad in the great depression, that at its worst, 25% of the U.S. population was unemployed! A lot of businesses closed down, imagine your high street with most the shops boarded up, and lots of people living on the street...

President Hoover worked very hard to help the country during this tough time. He created new projects to provide jobs and tried to help businesses get back on their feet.

Even though these were difficult years, Bert never stopped trying to improve things for the American people. Unfortunately, by the end of his first term, his policies were not effective enough and the country was still struggling with poverty in the great depression. Mainly for this reason, Bert massively lost the 1932 election to candidate Franklin D. Roosevelt.

After his presidency, Herbert Hoover continued to help others. He led food relief efforts during World War II and helped with reconstruction work after the war. He also wrote many books sharing his experiences and ideas.

# Franklin D. Roosevelt

**Born:**
Jan 30, 1882

**Birthplace:**
Hyde Park
New York

**Presidency:**
1933 - 1945

**Died:**
Apr 12, 1945

Franklin Delano Roosevelt, often known simply as FDR, was born on January 30, 1882, in Hyde Park, New York. He was born to a wealthy and well-known family, but even as a little boy, FDR knew that there was more to life than just money and fame. He was taught that it's more important to be kind, fair, and brave.

FDR was very bright and loved to learn. After finishing school, he went to Harvard University, one of the top universities in the United States. He studied history and economics and learned how to be a good leader.

In 1905, FDR married Eleanor Roosevelt, his fifth cousin once removed. She was smart, kind, and deeply cared about people.

They had six children together and were a strong team, both at home and in their work to help the nation.

In 1910, FDR decided to use his knowledge and skills to help make the world a better place. He entered politics and was elected to the New York State Senate. He was a Democrat, a member of one of the two major political parties in the United States.

In 1921, something happened that changed FDR's life forever. He was stricken with polio, a disease that made his legs weak and unable to move. It was a tough time for FDR, but he didn't let it stop him. He worked hard to regain his strength and, even though he couldn't walk without help, he continued to work for the people.

In 1932, during a time when the United States was facing a severe economic crisis called the Great Depression, FDR was elected the 32nd President. People were suffering, losing their jobs, and many didn't have enough food to eat. But FDR had a plan. He introduced the "New Deal," a set of programs aimed at giving people jobs, stabilizing the economy, and making life better for ordinary people.

FDR was a beacon of hope during some of the darkest times in American history. He served as President for four terms, longer than any other President.

He led the nation not only through the Great Depression but also through World War II, a devastating global conflict.
When World War II started in 1939, the whole world was in danger.
FDR was there to lead America. He had a tough job to do, but he was not afraid - he knew he had to make tough decisions to protect the people he loved.
FDR was a smart man. He knew that America needed to prepare for the war. So, he started programs to build more ships, planes, and weapons. He believed that even though America was not in the war yet, it was important to be ready and thank goodness he prepared for it.
In 1941, something terrible happened. The Japanese attacked Pearl Harbor, a place where America's navy was stationed. This led to America joining the war. FDR was sad but he knew he had to guide his country through these tough times.
FDR made a famous speech that day. He said December 7, 1941, was a "date which will live in infamy". He was strong and confident and wanted everyone in America to know that they could face this challenge together.
Throughout the war, FDR worked hard to keep America strong.

He worked with leaders from other countries, called allies, to make plans and decisions. He even travelled a long way to meet with these leaders - these meetings were called the Big Three summits and were held with Winston Churchill from Britain and Joseph Stalin from the USSR. Under FDR, the USA and other allies liberated countries such as France, The Netherlands, Belgium and Italy from the Nazis and for this, FDR's name is honored in countless places throughout Europe. FDR also planned how the USA could help rebuild those nations that suffered from WW2.

FDR's leadership was so strong that he was elected president four times! That's more than any other U.S. president in history. He was the only president to serve more than two terms because the people believed in him.

But the war was hard on FDR. His health started to decline. Sadly, before he could see the end of the war, FDR passed away in 1945. Even though he was no longer there, his spirit and his leadership inspired America to continue the fight.

FDR passed away on April 12, 1945, but his legacy continues to shine brightly. He showed us that no matter what challenges we face, with courage and determination, we can overcome them.

# Harry S. Truman

**Born:**
May 8, 1884

**Birthplace:**
Lamar
Missouri

**Presidency:**
1945 - 1953

**Died:**
Dec 26, 1972

Harry S. Truman was born on May 8, 1884, in Lamar, Missouri. His parents were farmers, and young Harry grew up working on the family farm. It wasn't an easy life, but it taught him about hard work and dedication. He was named "Harry" to honor his mother's brother, Harrison Young, and the "S" in his name doesn't stand for anything but honors both of his grandfathers.

Harry was a good student who loved to read, especially history and music. He went to high school but didn't go to college because his family needed his help on the farm. Later, he served in World War I, where he showed great bravery and leadership.

In 1919, Harry married his childhood sweetheart, Bess Wallace. They had one child, a daughter named Margaret.

Harry loved his family dearly and worked hard to provide for them.

After the war, Harry started a men's clothing store with a friend, but the business didn't succeed. He could have given up, but Harry was not a quitter. He decided to enter politics, and with the help of his war comrades and the Democratic Party, he was elected a county official.

In 1934, Harry was elected to the U.S. Senate. He was an honest and hard-working senator who did his best to help his country. People liked and trusted him, so much so that in 1944, he was chosen to be President Franklin D. Roosevelt's Vice President.

In 1945, President Roosevelt died, and Harry became the 33rd President of the United States. It was a challenging time, with World War II still ongoing. But Harry proved to be a strong leader. He finished off the war in Europe, with Germany's surrender and after intense fighting with Japan, and after their refusal to surrender, made the difficult decision to drop atomic bombs on Japan.

After the war, Harry worked hard to rebuild the country and the world.

Harry was also confronted with a new, upcoming issue, the Cold War.

The Cold War would dominate politics in the USA for the next 40 years. The USSR, led by Joseph Stalin was an ally during the war, but they had their own ideas for how they wanted to deal with Germany and rebuild war-torn nations - with a system called communism, a system very different from that of the USA. Harry saw the spread of communism as a threat and introduced what is known as the "Truman Doctrine," which promised to help countries threatened by communism.

Partly because of this, he also supported the Marshall Plan, helping Europe recover after the war. This plan gave lots of money to western European countries such as Britain, France, The Netherlands and even Germany, to ensure that the countries can become prosperous again and the population would not have to suffer for longer, but also so that they do not get influenced by the USSR and communism.

In 1948, Harry was elected President in his own right.

Everyone thought he would lose, but he proved them wrong with his "whistle-stop" campaign, traveling and speaking directly to the people. It was then that he earned the nickname "Give 'Em Hell Harry."

In 1948, Harry helped save the German capital, Berlin from starvation in what was to be called the Berlin Airlift, one of the first major Cold War events. In 1950, Harry also defended South Korea in the Korean War. After his presidency, Harry returned to his hometown in Missouri, where he enjoyed a quiet life, reading and walking. He died on December 26, 1972. He will always be remembered as a President who made tough decisions with courage and integrity, a true example of a leader who faced challenges head-on.

# Dwight D. Eisenhower

**Born:**
Oct 14, 1890

**Birthplace:**
Denison
Texas

**Presidency:**
1953 - 1961

**Died:**
Mar 28, 1969

Dwight D. Eisenhower, also known as "Ike," was born on October 14, 1890, in Denison, Texas. He was the third of seven boys in his family. His family wasn't wealthy, but they were rich in love and values. They taught young Ike the importance of hard work, honesty, and kindness.

As a boy, Ike was active and loved sports. He also loved to read, and his mother encouraged him to read books on history and government. When he wasn't playing or reading, he was helping with chores or working part-time jobs to support his family.

Ike attended the U.S. Military Academy at West Point and graduated in 1915. He was a good student and a strong leader, earning the respect of his fellow cadets.

He later married Mamie Geneva Doud in 1916, and they had two sons together.
During World War II, Ike rose to prominence as a brilliant military strategist. He was named Supreme Commander of the Allied Forces and led the successful D-Day invasion in 1944, a critical turning point in the war. The D-Day invasion involved landing lots of troops in mainland Europe for the first time in WW2 and undoubtedly helped the USA win the war. The scene has been remade in movies such as Saving Private Ryan amongst others.
After the war, Ike continued to serve his country. He became the first Supreme Commander of NATO, helping to keep peace in Europe. But his journey was not over yet. In 1952, Ike decided to run for President of the United States.
He was elected the 34th President in 1952 and served two terms. As President, Ike worked to promote peace and prosperity. He ended the Korean War, maintained peace during the Cold War, and supported civil rights. He also launched the Interstate Highway System, one of the largest public works projects in American history, which has helped Americans travel across the country ever since.
Ike was a popular President, admired for his calm and steady leadership.

He guided the nation with a steady hand during times of both peace and turmoil. Outside of work, Ike was an avid golfer and played the sport regularly during his presidency. He even had a putting green installed on the White House grounds so he could practice his golf game.

After serving two terms as President, he retired in 1961 and lived a quiet life in Gettysburg, Pennsylvania, until he passed away in 1969.

# John F. Kennedy

**Born:**
May 19, 1917

**Birthplace:**
Brookline
Massachussetts

**Presidency:**
1961 - 1963

**Died:**
Nov 22, 1963

John F. Kennedy, also known as "Jack" or JFK, was born on May 29, 1917, in Brookline, Massachusetts. He was the second of nine children in a lively and competitive family. His parents, Joseph and Rose Kennedy, taught him the importance of public service and encouraged him to be curious and ambitious. Jack was a charming and charismatic boy, although he often fell ill. Despite his health issues, he loved to read and play sports. He particularly enjoyed history and stories about heroic adventures.

After graduating from Harvard University in 1940, JFK joined the U.S. Navy during World War II. JFK served as a lieutenant in the U.S. Navy and he commanded a patrol torpedo boat (PT-109) in the Pacific.

In 1943, the PT-109 was struck by a Japanese destroyer, but JFK's leadership helped save the surviving crew members. They would swim to an island, where JFK even swam back to the wreckage to rescue an injured member and pull them to the island. JFK would swim to nearby islands to help find resources such as food and water for his crew. On the island, they waited until they were spotted by the crew of another U.S. ship. His heroic actions earned him the Navy and Marine Corps Medal, a high honor.

After the war, JFK decided to enter politics to help make the world a better place. He was elected to the U.S. House of Representatives in 1946 and the U.S. Senate in 1952. In 1953, he married Jacqueline Bouvier, and they had four children together.

JFK became the 35th President of the United States in 1961, making him the youngest person ever elected to the presidency. He was a powerful speaker, inspiring people with his words. His famous call, "Ask not what your country can do for you - ask what you can do for your country," encouraged Americans to contribute to the betterment of their country.

During his presidency, JFK faced many challenges, including the failed invasion of Cuba and the Cuban Missile Crisis, where he managed to avoid a nuclear war. He also supported the Civil Rights Movement and launched the space race with the goal of sending an American to the moon. He also supported Germany by travelling to Berlin when the infamous Berlin Wall was built.

JFK's life was tragically cut short on November 22, 1963, when he was assassinated by Lee Harvey Oswald in Dallas, Texas.

His death shocked the nation, but his legacy lives on. He inspired a new generation to public service and set the nation on a path towards equal rights and space exploration.

JFK announced the goal of landing a man on the moon before the end of the decade in 1961. This vision led to the Apollo program and ultimately resulted in the moon landing by the Apollo 11 mission in 1969, less than 5 months before the decade was out.

# Lyndon B. Johnson

**Born:**
Aug 27, 1908

**Birthplace:**
Gillespie
County
Texas

**Presidency:**
1963 - 1969

**Died:**
Jan 22, 1973

Lyndon B. Johnson, or LBJ as he was often called, was born on August 27, 1908, in a small farmhouse near Stonewall, Texas. He was the oldest of five children in a family that didn't have a lot of money but had plenty of love and determination. His parents taught him the importance of hard work and caring for others.

LBJ was also a bright and ambitious boy; even though his family couldn't afford much, he knew the importance of education. He worked his way through school, even taking a year off to teach Mexican-American children at a small Texas school. This experience deeply affected him, and he vowed to fight poverty and injustice.

After college, LBJ went into politics. He was first elected to the U.S. House of Representatives and then to the U.S. Senate.

In 1960, he was chosen as John F. Kennedy's running mate, and they won the election. As Vice President, LBJ was known for his hard work and dedication to improving the lives of everyday Americans.

When tragedy struck in November 1963, when President Kennedy was assassinated, LBJ was quickly sworn in as the 36th President of the United States. It was a difficult time for the nation, but LBJ was determined to carry on Kennedy's work.

As President, LBJ introduced what he called the "Great Society," a set of programs aimed at ending poverty and racial injustice. He signed the Civil Rights Act of 1964 and the Voting Rights Act of 1965, landmark laws that helped to end racial segregation and ensure voting rights for African Americans. LBJ also worked to improve education, healthcare, and the environment. But his presidency was also plagued by the Vietnam War, a controversial and unpopular war that led to widespread protests that began the counterculture in the USA, or maybe more popularly known as hippie culture.

In 1968, LBJ decided not to run for a second term as President. He returned to his Texas ranch, where he lived until his death in 1973.

# Richard Nixon

**Born:**
Jan 9, 1913

**Birthplace:**
Yorba Linda
California

**Presidency:**
1969 - 1974

**Died:**
Apr 22, 1994

Richard Milhous Nixon was born on January 9, 1913, in Yorba Linda, California. He was the second of five boys in his family. Growing up in a modest family, Richard learned early on about hard work and perseverance. His parents, Frank and Hannah Nixon, instilled in him a strong sense of duty and discipline.

Richard was a bright student who loved to learn. He excelled in school and went on to study at Whittier College and Duke University Law School. During World War II, he served in the U.S. Navy, demonstrating his dedication to his country.

After the war, Richard entered politics and was elected to the U.S. House of Representatives in 1946. In 1950, he won a seat in the U.S. Senate.

In 1952, he was chosen as Dwight D. Eisenhower's running mate, and they won the election, making Richard the Vice President of the United States.

In 1960, Richard ran for President but lost in a very close race to John F. Kennedy. However, he didn't give up. Richard made a political comeback and was elected the 37th President of the United States in 1968.

As President, Richard had to deal with the ongoing Vietnam War, and he worked to improve relations with China, a country that had shut themselves off from the western world till that point, and the USSR. He also established the Environmental Protection Agency and made progress in desegregation in the South.

Richard Nixon also famously met with Elvis Presley at the White House in 1970. The encounter took place in the Oval Office, where Presley expressed his concern about the influence of drugs on American youth and offered his assistance in promoting patriotism. The meeting is now famously captured in a photograph.

However, Richard's presidency was damaged by the Watergate scandal, a political scandal involving the Nixon administration's attempt to cover up a break-in at the Democratic National Committee headquarters.

As investigations continued, it became clear that Richard had been involved in the cover-up.
Faced with the possibility of impeachment, Nixon made the decision to resign from the presidency in 1974, the only U.S. President ever to do so. He spent the rest of his life working to repair his tarnished reputation, writing books, and advising future presidents before his death in 1994.
Richard Nixon's life teaches us about resilience and the consequences of our actions, especially that you can spend your whole life doing good, and that one bad action can ruin your whole reputation.
Richard achieved great things during his presidency, but it is often remembered for its unfortunate end.

# Gerald Ford

**Born:**
Jul 4, 1913

**Birthplace:**
Omaha
Nebraska

**Presidency:**
1974 - 1977

**Died:**
Dec 6, 2006

Gerald R. Ford was born as Leslie Lynch King Jr. on July 14, 1913, in Omaha, Nebraska. When he was only a few days old, his parents separated, and his mother moved to Grand Rapids, Michigan. She later remarried a man named Gerald R. Ford, and they began calling their son Gerald R. Ford Jr., even though his name was never officially changed until he was an adult.

Gerald grew up in Michigan as a very athletic and hardworking young man. He was an Eagle Scout, and played American football, where he was a center and a linebacker, and his team won two national championships during his time there. Gerald was even offered contracts to play football for the Detroit Lions and the Green Bay Packers, but he had different plans and decided to study law at Yale University.

During World War II, Gerald served in the U.S. Navy, demonstrating bravery and leadership.

After the war, he returned to Grand Rapids, where he married Elizabeth Bloomer, also known as Betty Ford. They had four children together.

In 1948, Gerald was elected to the U.S. House of Representatives, where he served for 25 years. He was well-respected and known for his honesty and dedication to service.

In 1973, Vice President Spiro Agnew resigned, and President Richard Nixon chose Gerald to replace him. This was a time of turmoil and uncertainty because of the Watergate scandal involving President Nixon. Then, in August 1974, Nixon also resigned, and Gerald suddenly became the 38th President of the United States. This made him the first person to assume the presidency without being elected as President or Vice President. He became Vice President under Richard Nixon in 1973 after the resignation of Spiro Agnew, and then assumed the presidency in 1974 after Nixon resigned due to the Watergate scandal.

Gerald's presidency was a time of healing for the nation.

One of his first acts as President was to pardon Richard Nixon, clearing his name of all accusations of crime in the scandal, a controversial decision, but one Gerald believed was necessary for the country to move forward.

He worked towards ending the Vietnam War and dealing with an economic crisis.

Despite not being elected to the position, Gerald served the remainder of Richard Nixon's term with integrity and steadiness.

He ran for election in 1976 but was narrowly defeated by Jimmy Carter.

After leaving the presidency, Gerald remained active in public life and worked on causes he cared about until his death in 2006.

# Jimmy Carter

**Born:**
Oct 1, 1924

**Birthplace:**
Plains
Georgia

**Presidency:**
1977 - 1981

James Earl Carter Jr., known as Jimmy Carter, was born on October 1, 1924, in Plains, Georgia. He grew up in a house without electricity or indoor plumbing, and his family worked hard on their peanut farm. This humble upbringing taught him the values of hard work, honesty, and caring for others.

Young Jimmy was a bright and curious boy who loved to read. He also enjoyed working on the farm and spending time outdoors. These experiences shaped his love for nature and his commitment to conservation later in life.

After high school, Carter attended the U.S. Naval Academy and graduated in 1946. He then served in the Navy, where he worked on submarines.

During his time in the Navy, he married Rosalynn Smith, and they went on to have four children together.

After his father's death, Carter returned to Plains to take over the family farm. He became involved in local politics and was elected governor of Georgia in 1970. As governor, he focused on improving education and civil rights.

In 1976, Carter was elected the 39th President of the United States. His presidency was marked by a focus on human rights, peace, and conservation. He established the Department of Energy and the Department of Education, and he worked towards peace in the Middle East, which led to the historic Camp David Accords.

However, Carter faced many challenges during his presidency, including an energy crisis, high inflation, and the Iran hostage crisis. He ran for re-election in 1980 but was defeated by Ronald Reagan.

After leaving office, Carter didn't retire quietly. He and Rosalynn founded The Carter Center, an organization dedicated to promoting peace and public health worldwide. He also became involved with Habitat for Humanity, building houses for those in need. In 2002, Carter was awarded the Nobel Peace Prize for his humanitarian work.

# Ronald Reagan

**Born:**
Feb 6, 1911

**Birthplace:**
Tampico
Illinois

**Presidency:**
1981 - 1989

**Died:**
Jun 5, 2004

Once upon a time, there was a boy named Ronald Reagan who was born on February 6, 1911, in a small town in Illinois. Ronald was very active as a child; he loved swimming, sports, and acting in school plays. He had a saying that he learned from his mother, "We can always find something to be thankful for," which would guide him throughout his life.

After he graduated from high school, Ronald went to Eureka College, where he studied economics and sociology. He was a very involved student, participating in many activities like football, track, and acting in plays. After college, he moved to Iowa and became a sports radio announcer. With his clear, strong voice, he was really good at making listeners feel as if they were right there in the stadium.

His career took an exciting turn when he became a Hollywood actor. Ronald starred in over 50 films and became quite popular, probably his most famous role was George Gipp in "Knute Rockne, All American." In Hollywood, he also became the president of the Screen Actors Guild, the union for actors, where he fought for the rights of his fellow actors. In this role of helping others, he grew deeply interested in politics and how he could help others on a larger scale.

He often talked about how much he loved America and believed in its potential. He thought the government should have less control over people's lives and that people should have more freedom to make their own choices.

In 1966, Ronald was elected governor of California. He worked hard to help the state and its people, gaining a lot of popularity. After serving two terms, Ronald had a new goal in mind: he wanted to be the president of the United States.

In 1980, his dream came true. Ronald Reagan became the 40th president of the United States. He served two terms and during his presidency, he was known for his good humor, optimism, and belief in America's greatness.

He worked to make the economy stronger and to end the Cold War with the USSR, a period when the United States and Russia were often on the edge of conflict.

He confronted the USSR about the Berlin Wall, telling them to tear it down in a now famous speech.

The Berlin Wall was torn down just two years after Ronald's speech, and soon after that, the Cold War ended.

After he retired, Ronald announced in 1994 that he had Alzheimer's disease, a condition that affects the brain. But he remained hopeful and strong, writing in a letter to the American people, "I now begin the journey that will lead me into the sunset of my life. I know that for America there will always be a bright dawn ahead."

And so, Ronald Reagan, from the small town in Illinois, will always be remembered as an actor, governor, and president who loved his country deeply and believed in the power of hope, freedom, and gratitude.

# George H. W. Bush

**Born:**
Jun 12, 1924

**Birthplace:**
Milton
Massachussetts

**Presidency:**
1989 - 1993

**Died:**
Nov 30, 2018

Once upon a time, in a big city called Milton, Massachusetts, a child named George Herbert Walker Bush was born on June 12, 1924. George grew up in a large family with three brothers, one sister, and very loving parents. As a child, he loved baseball and was a very dedicated and responsible boy. When George was just 18 years old, he chose to serve his country in World War II. He became the youngest pilot in the United States Navy at that time. He was brave and flew in 58 combat missions. In one of those missions, his plane was hit by enemy fire, but George successfully parachuted out and was rescued at sea. He was awarded the Distinguished Flying Cross for his bravery. After the war, George went to Yale University, where he was a very good student.

Bush also had a passion for baseball and was a skilled player. During his time at Yale University, he played first base and was the captain of the Yale Bulldogs baseball team. His team reached the first College World Series in 1947. After graduation, he moved to Texas and started a successful oil company.

George's heart was not only in business but also in public service. He was elected to the U.S. House of Representatives, where he worked hard for the people of Texas. Later, he served as the United States Ambassador to the United Nations and as the Director of the Central Intelligence Agency. He also was Vice President under Ronald Reagan for eight years.

Then, in 1988, George achieved his dream: he became the 41st president of the United States. As president, he was dedicated to making America a "kinder and gentler" nation. He signed a law that protects people with disabilities, and he played a key role in ending the Cold War peacefully.

One of the most memorable moments of his presidency was when he led America and a global coalition to liberate Kuwait in the Gulf War. This victory reinforced the United States' commitment to establishing peace and stability in the world.

After serving one term as president, George retired from politics. But his dedication to public service lived on in his children.
His son George W. Bush also became president, and his son Jeb Bush became the governor of Florida.
Even in his later years, George continued to inspire many with his spirit of service. He even celebrated his 90th birthday in 2014 by going skydiving. It was not his first time skydiving, as he had previously made jumps to commemorate his 80th and 85th birthdays as well. This adventurous activity showcased his lively spirit and zest for life.

# Bill Clinton

**Born:**
Aug 19, 1946

**Birthplace:**
Hope
Arkansas

**Presidency:**
1993 - 2001

Once upon a time in a small town called Hope, Arkansas, a boy named William Jefferson Blythe IV was born on August 19, 1946. His father had died before he was born, and his mother had to go away for nursing school, so he was raised by his grandparents for a few years. When his mother returned, she married a man named Roger Clinton, and young William later decided to take his stepfather's last name, becoming known as Bill Clinton.

Bill was a good student and loved playing the saxophone. He was so good at it that he even considered becoming a professional musician. But when he was a teenager, he met President John F. Kennedy, and that meeting changed his life. Bill decided that he wanted to work in public service and help others.

Bill studied hard in school and won a scholarship to the prestigious Georgetown University in Washington, D.C. He continued his studies in England at Oxford University and then returned to the U.S. to study law at Yale University. There, he met a smart and ambitious woman named Hillary Rodham. They fell in love and got married.

After finishing his studies, Bill returned to Arkansas, where he became a law professor. Soon, he decided to run for public office. He became the youngest governor of Arkansas and served in this role for many years, working hard to improve education and the economy in his state.

In 1992, Bill Clinton ran for president, and he won. He became the 42nd president of the United States. During his presidency, he focused on the economy, and more jobs were created than ever before. He also worked hard to make peace in other parts of the world.

Even after his presidency, Bill remained active. He and his wife, Hillary, started the Clinton Foundation to address global challenges like health, climate change, and economic inequality.

# George W. Bush

**Born:**
Jul 6, 1946

**Birthplace:**
New Haven
Connecticut

**Presidency:**
2001 - 2009

In a lively city called New Haven, Connecticut, on July 6, 1946, a boy named George Walker Bush was born. George was the first child in a big, loving family. His father, George H. W. Bush, was also a president, making them only the second father-son president duo in American history!

As a young boy, George was an excellent athlete and loved playing baseball. He was known for his fun-loving spirit and warm heart. His family moved to Texas when he was still young, and he came to love the wide open spaces and friendly people there.

George was a good student. He went to Yale University, just like his father, and later attended Harvard Business School.

After finishing his studies, he returned to Texas, where he started his own oil and gas business. He loved Texas so much he even bought a baseball team, the Texas Rangers! However, George also felt a strong call to public service, like his father. He ran for governor of Texas and won, serving for two terms. As governor, he worked on improving education, healthcare, and the state's economy.

In the year 2000, George decided to follow in his father's footsteps and run for president. After a very close election, he became the 43rd president of the United States. He served two terms as president. His presidency was marked by significant events, such as the 9/11 terrorist attacks, which led to the wars in Afghanistan and Iraq. He also focused on education, passing a law called No Child Left Behind to improve schools.

After his presidency, George returned to Texas and took up painting as a hobby. He even published a book of his artwork! He also started the George W. Bush Presidential Center, which works on issues like education reform, global health, and human freedom.

# Barack Obama

**Born:**
Aug 4, 1961

**Birthplace:**
Honolulu
Hawaii

**Presidency:**
2009 - 2017

On a sunny day in Hawaii, on August 4, 1961, a child named Barack Hussein Obama was born. Barack's name meant "blessed" in Swahili, a language from Kenya where his father was from. His mother was from Kansas, making Barack mixed race.

As a child in Hawaii, Barack loved to play basketball and read books. At age 7, he was sent to Indonesia for 3 years, before moving to New York to attend Columbia University. Then, he moved to Chicago, a city that would become very dear to him. There, he worked to help people who had lost their jobs and were struggling.

Feeling a strong urge to do more for people, Barack decided to study law. He attended Harvard Law School and became the first African American president of the Harvard Law Review, which was a very big deal.

It was also at law school where he met his future wife, Michelle.
After finishing his studies, Barack returned to Chicago. He taught law and worked as a community organizer. He also started his political career in the Illinois State Senate. Barack's passion for helping people and his talent for making inspiring speeches made many people believe in him.
In 2004, Barack gave a speech at the Democratic National Convention that made him famous across the country. He talked about unity, hope, and the American dream. Two years later, he decided to run for president. In 2006, Barack won a Grammy Award for Best Spoken Word Album for his audiobook "Dreams from My Father."

In 2008, Barack Obama made history when he became the 44th president of the United States and the first African American to hold this office. He was president for two terms. During his presidency, he worked on health care reform to make healthcare more affordable, improving the economy, and environmental issues.
Barack Obama outside office hours had a strong passion for basketball. He played the sport in high school and continued to play recreationally during his presidency.

He even installed a basketball court in the White House grounds, allowing him to shoot hoops and play pickup games with friends and staff members.

After his presidency, Barack remained active in public life. He and Michelle started the Obama Foundation to inspire and empower future leaders around the world. Barack Obama's journey from Hawaii to the White House shows us that with hope, hard work, and a desire to help others, anyone can achieve their dreams.

# Donald Trump

**Born:**
Jun 14, 1946

**Birthplace:**
Queens
New York City

**Presidency:**
2017 - 2021

Once upon a time in a place called Queens, New York, a boy named Donald John Trump was born on June 14, 1946. Donald was the fourth of five children in a bustling family. His father, Fred Trump, was a successful real estate developer and taught Donald all about the business world.

Donald was an energetic boy who loved to dream big. To help him focus his energy, his parents sent him to a military academy for school where he learned about discipline and leadership. After he finished high school, he studied economics at the Wharton School of the University of Pennsylvania.

After graduating, Donald joined his father's company and started to make his own mark in the world of real estate. He built tall buildings, hotels, and golf courses all over the world.

One of his most famous projects is the impressive 58-story Trump Tower in New York City. Donald was also famous for his television show, "The Apprentice", where people competed for a job in his company. For his role in the show, he has a star on the Hollywood Walk of Fame. It was awarded to him in 2007 for his work as a producer and host of the reality TV show "The Apprentice." The star is located on Hollywood Boulevard in Los Angeles.

Donald Trump made cameo appearances in several movies and TV shows, including "Home Alone 2: Lost in New York," "Zoolander," and "Sex and the City."

But Donald wanted to do more than just real estate and showbiz. He decided to run for president of the United States. Many people didn't think he could win because he had never held a political office (for example, a senator) before, which has been basically neccessary for previous presidencies. But Donald nonetheless believed in himself and did his best to win the people's vote.

In 2016, Donald Trump won against Hillary Clinton and became the 45th president of the United States. During his presidency, Donald focused on issues like immigration and unfair trade.

He also tried to disarm North Korea by meeting with Kim Jong Un several times. He also partially built a wall at the U.S.-Mexico border and had to deal with a global pandemic.

After serving one term as president, Donald lost the election to Joe Biden and went back to his business.

His time in the White House was an important chapter in his life.

Donald Trump's story, from a boy in Queens to a businessman, TV star, and president, shows us that believing in yourself and dreaming big can take you to places you never imagined.

# Joe Biden

**Born:**
Nov 20, 1942

**Birthplace:**
Scranton
Pennsylvania

**Presidency:**
2021 -

In the small city of Scranton, Pennsylvania, a boy named Joseph Robinette Biden Jr. was born on November 20, 1942. His family called him "Joe" around the house and so Joe would continue to use that as his name. Joe wasn't born in a hospital, but at home, in a really small and cozy apartment.

As a child, Joe loved playing football and baseball. But there was something that made his childhood a bit difficult: he had a stutter, which made speaking clearly a challenge. But Joe was a fighter. He worked hard to overcome his stutter, practicing in front of a mirror until he could speak without stumbling over his words.

Joe's family moved to Delaware when he was 10. He went to the University of Delaware for college and then law school at Syracuse University.

After graduating, he worked as a lawyer and also as a city councilor, helping to make decisions for his local community.

But Joe had bigger dreams. At just 29, he was elected as one of Delaware's U.S. senators. Tragically, just a few weeks later, his wife and young daughter died in a car accident. Joe was devastated, but he decided to keep going for his two sons, who survived the accident.

Joe served in the U.S. Senate for a long time, working on issues like crime, climate change, and foreign relations. In 2008, he was elected as vice president under President Barack Obama. They worked together for eight years, becoming close friends.

Then, in 2020, Joe decided to run for president. He won the election, becoming the 46th president of the United States, becoming the oldest president at age 78 to take office. His presidency is still ongoing, and he has faced national issues such as the pandemic.

Joe Biden's journey from a small boy with a stutter to the president of the United States shows us that with determination, hard work, and resilience, we can overcome any obstacles we face.

***Who will be the next president to follow after Joe?***

Printed in Great Britain
by Amazon